D1194172

# Extreme
# DOWNHILL
# SKI RACING

Virginia Loh-Hagan

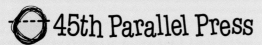
# 45th Parallel Press

Published in the United States of America by Cherry Lake Publishing
Ann Arbor, Michigan
www.cherrylakepublishing.com

Content Adviser: Liv Williams, Editor, www.iLivExtreme.com
Reading Adviser: Marla Conn, ReadAbility, Inc.
Photo Credits: ©Samo Vidic/Red Bull Content Pool, 5; ©Erich Spiess/Red Bull Content Pool, 6; ©Olaf Pignataro/Red Bull Content Pool, 8; ©Andreas Gall/Red Bull Content Pool, 11; ©Denis Pepin/Shutterstock.com, 13; ©ASP Red Bull/Red Bull Content Pool, 15; ©Mono Collective/Shutterstock.com, 17; ©Olaf Pignataro/Red Bull Content Pool, 19; ©JEAN-CHRISTOPHE BOTT/EPA/Newscom, 21; ©WENN Ltd /Alamy Stock Photo, 22; ©Mitch Gunn/Shutterstock.com, 25; ©Erich Spiess/Red Bull Content Pool, 27; ©Maxim Blinkov/Shutterstock.com, 29; ©Trusjom/Shutterstock.com, multiple interior pages; ©Kues/Shutterstock.com, multiple interior pages

**45th Parallel Press** is an imprint of Cherry Lake Publishing.

Library of Congress Cataloging-in-Publication Data

Names: Loh-Hagan, Virginia.
Title: Extreme downhill ski racing / by Virginia Loh-Hagan.
Description: Ann Arbor : Cherry Lake Publishing, [2016] | Series: Nailed it!
  | Includes bibliographical references and index.
Identifiers: LCCN 2015049732| ISBN 9781634710923 (hardcover) | ISBN
  9781634711913 (pdf) | ISBN 9781634712903 (paperback) | ISBN 9781634713894
  (ebook)
Subjects: LCSH: Downhill ski racing--Juvenile literature. | Extreme
  sports--Juvenile literature.
Classification: LCC GV854.9.R3 L65 2016 | DDC 796.93/5--dc23
LC record available at http://lccn.loc.gov/2015049732

Printed in the United States of America
Corporate Graphics Inc.

## ABOUT THE AUTHOR

Dr. Virginia Loh-Hagan is an author, university professor, former classroom teacher, and curriculum designer. She likes going downhill—in her car. She lives in San Diego with her very tall husband and very naughty dogs. To learn more about her, visit www.virginialoh.com.

# Table of Contents

# Racing Against Time

*Who are some famous downhill ski racers? How are they unstoppable?*

Scott Macartney went down an icy slope. He skied 90 miles (145 kilometers) an hour. In two minutes, he skied 3,000 feet (914 meters). He made sharp turns. He made big jumps. He flew in the air. Something went wrong. The wind twisted him. He couldn't fix himself. He landed on his hip. His head slammed into ice. His helmet flew off. He slid 200 feet (61 m).

His brain was bruised. But he got better. He returned to Austria to race in the Hahnenkamm. It's the most extreme downhill ski race.

He's unstoppable. He was selected for the U.S. Ski Team. He competed in two Olympics. He said, "It has been an incredible ride."

Bode Miller is a downhill racing champion. He's won the most skiing medals in the Winter Olympics. But he's never won the Hahnenkamm. He has tried several times. He said, "It breaks your heart a little bit as a racer."

Some race course jumps are as big as a football field.

Extreme downhill racers make tight turns and big jumps.

Miller made several mistakes at the Hahnenkamm. He came down fast. He jumped. His ski came underneath him. He got turned around. He said, "That mistake is just too big of a mistake. It just cost me way, way too much time." Miller keeps training. He keeps trying.

Every second counts. Downhill racers race against time. It's a high-speed sport.

Lindsey Vonn is the most successful female downhill ski racer. She's won many races. She said, "I like to do things fast. I'm pretty fearless all around."

**NAILED IT!**

## Spotlight Biography: Takeshi Suzuki

Takeshi Suzuki is a Japanese extreme downhill racer. He's a Paralympic athlete. Paralympics are games for professional athletes with disabilities. Suzuki was getting off a bus. He was on his way home from school. A truck cut off his legs. He was eight years old. Seventeen years later to the day, he won gold and bronze medals. He uses a sit-ski. It's a seat attached to skis. He always touches his skis before a race. He was born and raised in a skiing resort in northern Japan. He started competing at a young age. His parents supported him. He said, "They have brought me up as a normal child even after I was disabled. I want to hang the medal around their necks."

Training is a big part of downhill racing.

She's had many accidents. She's had many injuries. She's hurt her hips, knees, back, and brain. But she keeps skiing.

She crashed in a race. She rolled down the mountain. She skied through a gate. She hurt her knee. She recovered. She skied again. She crashed again. She said, "Winning is always a great feeling. But it's mostly about the challenge."

Ski racers fall. They get back up.

"Downhill racers race against time."

# Racing Downhill

*What is extreme downhill racing like? What is a fall line?*

Extreme downhill racing is a specific kind of **alpine** skiing. Alpine refers to high mountains.

Extreme ski races are downhill. They are the longest races. Ski racers ski over 90 miles (145 km) per hour. The skier with the fastest time wins. Downhill racing is the fastest land sport that doesn't use a **motor**. A motor is an engine. It moves things.

Johan Clarey set a speed record. He raced downhill at 100.6 miles (162 km) per hour. He said, "It's a good feeling, and it wasn't scary."

Ski race courses have long paths. They start at the tops of mountains. They start on **piste**. Piste means the paths are groomed. They're smooth. They have difficult turns. They have bumps. Ski racers can catch air.

Gates help mark the path. Paths have safety nets and padding. Courses are sprayed with water or salt. This increases icing. Icing increases speed.

A ski race is a single downhill run.

Racers follow the **fall line**. It's the path of a falling object down a slope. It's the fastest path down a slope. Skiers use this line.

## Advice from the Field: Hubertus von Hohenlohe

Hubertus von Hohenlohe is not a typical extreme downhill racer. He's also a German pop singer and a prince. His grandmother was half Mexican. He was born in Mexico. But he mainly lived in Austria. He's a citizen in both countries. He represented Mexico in the Olympics. He's the second-oldest athlete to compete. He's never medaled. He's never finished better than 26th place. But he has fun. He wears costumes while skiing. He wore a Mariachi ski suit. He wants to win "best dressed." He advises athletes to be grateful. He said, "I didn't think anything can happen. Now I have three broken knees, one broken leg, one broken hand. Don't take anything for granted."

Ski resorts create courses for racers.

Ski racers tuck themselves in. They make themselves small and tight. They squat. They lean forward. They hold their arms against their sides. This makes them race faster. Tucking also decreases **drag**. Drag is a pulling feeling.

Racers have special gear. Their skis are longer than other skis. They're more stable at faster speeds. Their skis have round tips. Their ski poles are bent. Poles curve around the body.

Racers protect their bodies. They wear skintight suits. They wear helmets and pads.

Skiers use gravity to help race downhill.

# From Europe to the World

*How did downhill racing develop? Who helped develop the sport?*

Skiing is over 4,500 years old. Early humans strapped wood to their feet. They skied from one place to another. This became **cross-country** skiing. They walked with skis.

In 1921, Arnold Lunn developed the rules for downhill ski racing. He hosted the first races. He changed how people thought about skiing. Lunn introduced downhill racing into the 1936 Olympics.

Lunn himself didn't race. He had an accident climbing mountains. His right leg was 2 inches (5 centimeters) shorter than his left.

In 1927, the first U.S. downhill race took place in New Hampshire. Charles N. Proctor won. It took him 21 minutes. The slope was on a road used by **carriages**. Carriages were cars pulled by horses. The course was steep. It had many twists. It went through heavy woods.

Cave drawings of skiing were found in Sweden.

# Extreme Downhill Racing: Know the Lingo

**Beeline:** going straight down a hill with no turns

**Bluebird:** blue sky, no clouds, perfect skiing day

**Bomber:** a person who skis too fast or out of control

**Brain bucket:** helmet

**Cruise:** ski casually down an easy slope

**Dump:** huge snowfall

**Edging:** controlling turns with the edges of your skis

**Face shot:** skiing fast down a hill and having snow fly in your face

**French fries:** skiing with skis parallel to one another

**Milk run:** first ski run of the day

**Powder:** fresh, dry snow

**Schuss:** ski straight downhill very fast with skis parallel

**Tearing it up:** skiing well

**Whiteout:** not being able to see because of snow or fog

**Yard sale:** wiping out and having clothes and gear go flying everywhere

Ski equipment got better. Ski racers can now go even faster.

Proctor helped develop the first **chairlift**. Chairlifts bring ski racers to the tops of slopes. This saves them time and energy. Skiers don't have to climb up. They could ski many times. Chairlifts made ski racing more popular.

# Crash and Burn

*What are some risks of extreme downhill racing? What are some examples of extreme downhill racing injuries?*

It's easy to get injured when skiing. Injuries can be due to lack of skill. Crashes cause most injuries.

Brian Stemmle crashed into a safety net. His hips ripped open. A body organ exploded. His face was cut up. He slept for five days. He survived. He continued to race.

Matthias Lanzinger jumped. He slammed into a gate. He broke his left leg. He tumbled to a stop. His ski wouldn't release. His broken leg got twisted. Doctors had to cut off his leg.

Marcus Sandell raced on a **glacier**. A glacier is an ice mountain. Sandell crashed into large rocks. He lived. But he lost one of his kidneys.

Downhill ski racers race at top speeds. Sometimes they struggle to maintain control.

T. J. Lanning lost control for a second. He skied through a gate. He flipped forward. His left leg pointed in the wrong

Crashes are part of downhill racing.

Downhill racers ski down different mountains around the world. Some mountains are more dangerous than others.

direction. His ski was still attached. He broke his leg and knee. He broke neck bones. He recovered. He became a coach for the U.S. Ski Team.

He said, "I'm lucky to be able to be skiing. But the thought of crashing at 80 miles an hour again definitely goes through my mind."

Aksel Lund Svindal jumped. He crashed. His ski gashed his back. He almost bled to death. He recovered. He continued racing.

## That Happened?!?

Sheregesh, Russia is a popular winter resort. Winters are cold and snowy. That didn't stop 1,835 people from over 54 different places from wearing swimsuits. They got a world record. It was for the greatest number of participants in an almost-naked downhill ski run. They broke their own 2013 record of 500 people. These skiers went down a 1,640-foot (500 m) slope. Officials checked to make sure people weren't wearing too many clothes. More than 50 cameras recorded the event. Photos were taken from the air. This was so participants could be counted. The organizer said, "We want Sheregesh to be known as the place where people love having fun and sharing it with each other, where it's all about laughter and jokes."

Silvano Beltrametti was in a high-speed crash.
It **paralyzed** him. He can't move from the waist down.
He skied off the course. His skis crashed into a safety net.
He landed on a rock. He broke his back.

Ski racers need to be skilled. This is their real protection.
They can't make mistakes. A mistake could cause injury
or death.

Racers risk running into other racers. Their gear could
fail. They battle cold weather. They battle strong winds.
They battle **avalanches**.

Ski racers have safety nets, padding, and helmets.

# Future of Extreme Ski Racing

*What are some extreme competitions for extreme downhill racing? What are some variations of extreme downhill racing?*

Downhill racers are extreme. They go quickly down steep slopes. But some ski racers need more.

Skimeister is an extreme competition. First, skiers cross-country ski up a steep hill. Second, they downhill ski. Third, they bike to the finish line.

The Crashed Ice competition promotes ice cross downhill. It's downhill skating on an iced track. The track has walls. It has sharp turns. It has drops of over 200 feet (61 m).

It's about 1,500 feet (457 m) long. Participants wear ice skates instead of skis. They race four at a time. They push. They slide. They sprint. Andrew Bergeson loves this sport. He said, "It incorporates all the things I like: hitting people, skating, and fast speeds."

There are different versions of downhill ski racing.

Ski racers go quickly down a mountain with only boots and skis between them and the snow.

Some Norwegians played the first known game of downhill soccer skiing. Two teams raced downhill. They passed a soccer ball. The goal was at the slope's bottom.

## When Extreme Is Too Extreme!

Yak skiing developed in India. A yak is an animal. It's like a cow. A skier is at the bottom of a slope. The skier is roped to a yak by a pulley. The yak is at the top of the slope. The skier shakes a bucket of nuts. The skier quickly puts the bucket on the ground. This makes the yak race downhill. The yak wants the food. The skier shoots forward at top speeds. Peter Dorje is Tibetan. He created yak skiing. He advises, "Never shake the bucket of nuts before you're tied to the yak rope, though. If you shake the bucket too soon, you'll be flattened by two hairy tons of behemoth." Behemoth means a big beast.

Downhill ski racing isn't the only way to be extreme on the mountain.

Snow kayaking is another sport. Participants race with **kayaks** instead of skis. Kayaks are small, narrow boats. Participants paddle downhill. They do it in a kayak.

Downhill longboarders go down mountains at high speeds. Participants don't use brakes. They don't use safety nets. They use ski racing skills. They tuck themselves in.

Henrik May developed sand skiing. Sand skiers race using skis. They do it on large hills of sand.

Downhill skiers look for the next challenge.

# Did You Know?

- Hammarbybacken is a small ski resort. It's in Stockholm, Sweden. It has a man-made slope. The slope is 307 feet (93.5 m) high. It's built on top of a garbage dump.

- The word ski comes from the Norwegian word skío. Skio means "a piece of wood."

- Simone Origone has a world record. He's the fastest ski racer. He skied 156.2 miles (251.4 km) per hour. He said, "I am thrilled to be the fastest man on earth without a motor."

- Extreme downhill racing burns around 350 to 400 calories per hour.

- Paralympic ski racing started after World War II. Injured soldiers wanted to ski. So they found a way.

- Bill Johnson stole a car. He was 17 years old. He was known to be a good skier. He was sent to ski school instead of prison. He never stole again. Instead, he won an Olympic gold medal.

- In 1521, Denmark and Sweden went to war. People needed to carry hurt soldiers. Cloth was stretched between two skis. That's the origin of the word stretcher.

- There's a patron saint of skiers. It's St. Bernard of Montjoux. He takes care of skiers. St. Bernard dogs are named after him.

# Consider This!

TAKE A POSITION! Some people criticize sports like extreme ski racing. Skiing is expensive. So some people think it's snobby. They think it's too dangerous. They think it shouldn't count as a sport. Do you think extreme ski racing is a sport or not? Argue your point with reasons and evidence.

SAY WHAT? There are different types of ski racing. The 45th Parallel Press has books about extreme snow skiing and extreme ice cross downhill. Read these books and compare these sports to extreme ski racing. What are the similarities and differences between these extreme sports?

THINK ABOUT IT! Climate change is changing the weather. It's changing snow. Learn more about climate change. How do you think climate change affects extreme ski racing? What happens to ski resorts if there's little to no snow? What happens to winter sports if there is little to no snow?

SEE A DIFFERENT SIDE! Some people think extreme ski racing is too dangerous for children and teens. It's been called a "death race on ice." What do you think are the issues? Examine the risks and dangers.

# Learn More: Resources

### PRIMARY SOURCES

*The Thin Line*, a documentary about downhill ski racing (Rush HD and Jalbert Productions, 2008).

### SECONDARY SOURCES

Burns, Kylie. *Alpine and Freestyle Skiing*. New York: Crabtree Publishing Company, 2010.

Dann, Sarah. *Lindsey Vonn*. New York: Crabtree Publishing Company, 2013.

Firestone, Mary. *Extreme Downhill Skiing Moves*. Mankato, MN: Capstone High-Interest Books, 2004.

### WEB SITES

International Ski Federation: www.fis-ski.com

United States Ski and Snowboard Association: http://ussa.org

United States Ski Team: http://usskiteam.com

# Glossary

**avalanches** (AV-uh-lanch-iz) when snow flows quickly down a slope

**alpine** (AL-pine) related to high mountains

**carriages** (KEHR-ij-iz) cars that are pulled by horses

**chairlift** (CHEHR-lift) a system that takes skiers to the top of a slope

**cross-country** (kraws-KUN-tree) running or walking on flat land for a long time

**drag** (DRAG) resistance, the pulling feeling

**fall line** (FAWL LINE) the path of a falling object down a slope

**glacier** (GLAY-shur) a mountain of ice

**kayaks** (KYE-aks) small, narrow boats that are propelled by a double paddle

**motor** (MOH-tur) an engine that moves things like a car or motorcycle

**paralyzed** (PAR-uh-lized) unable to move

**piste** (PEEST) a groomed or man-made ski course

# Index